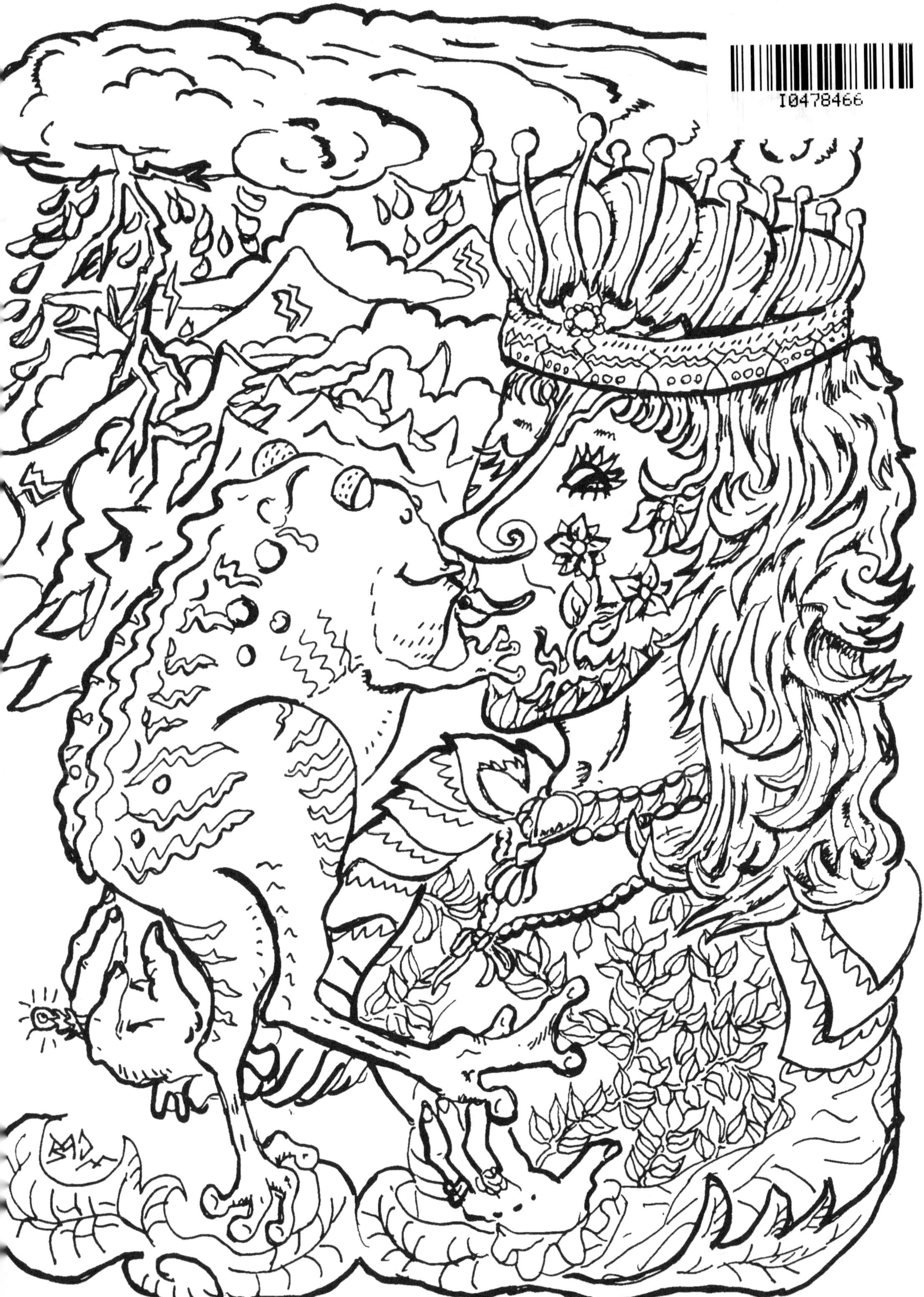

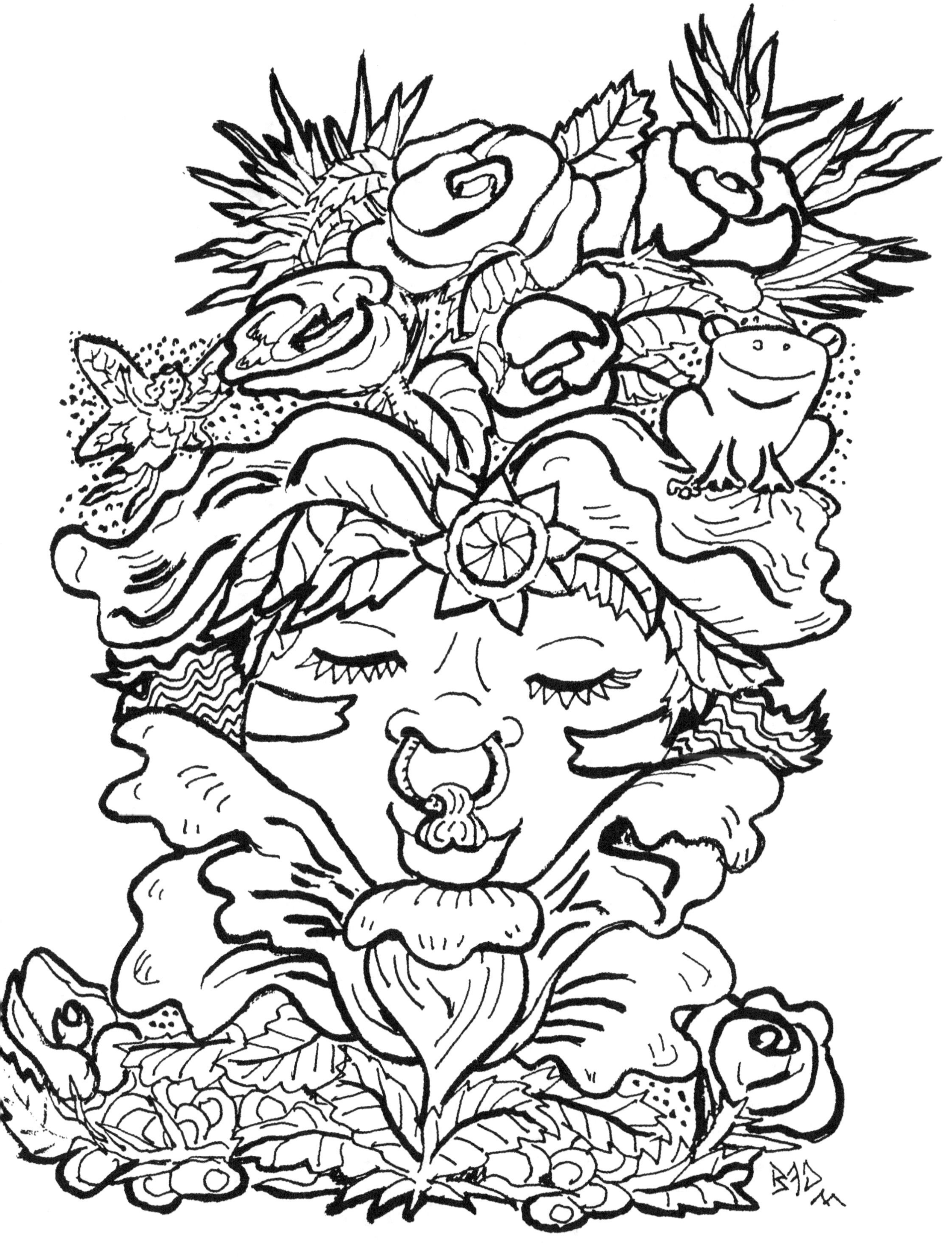

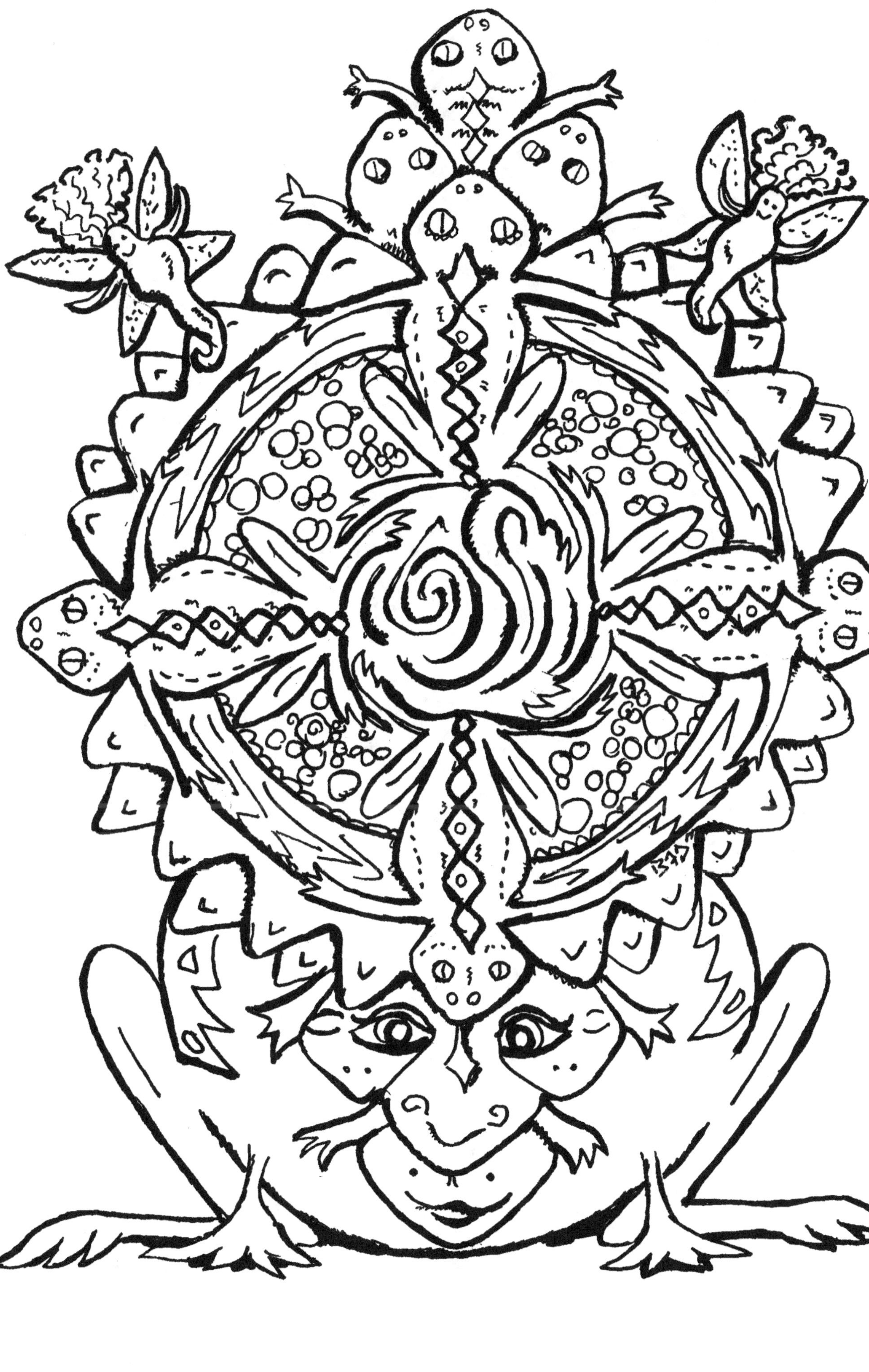

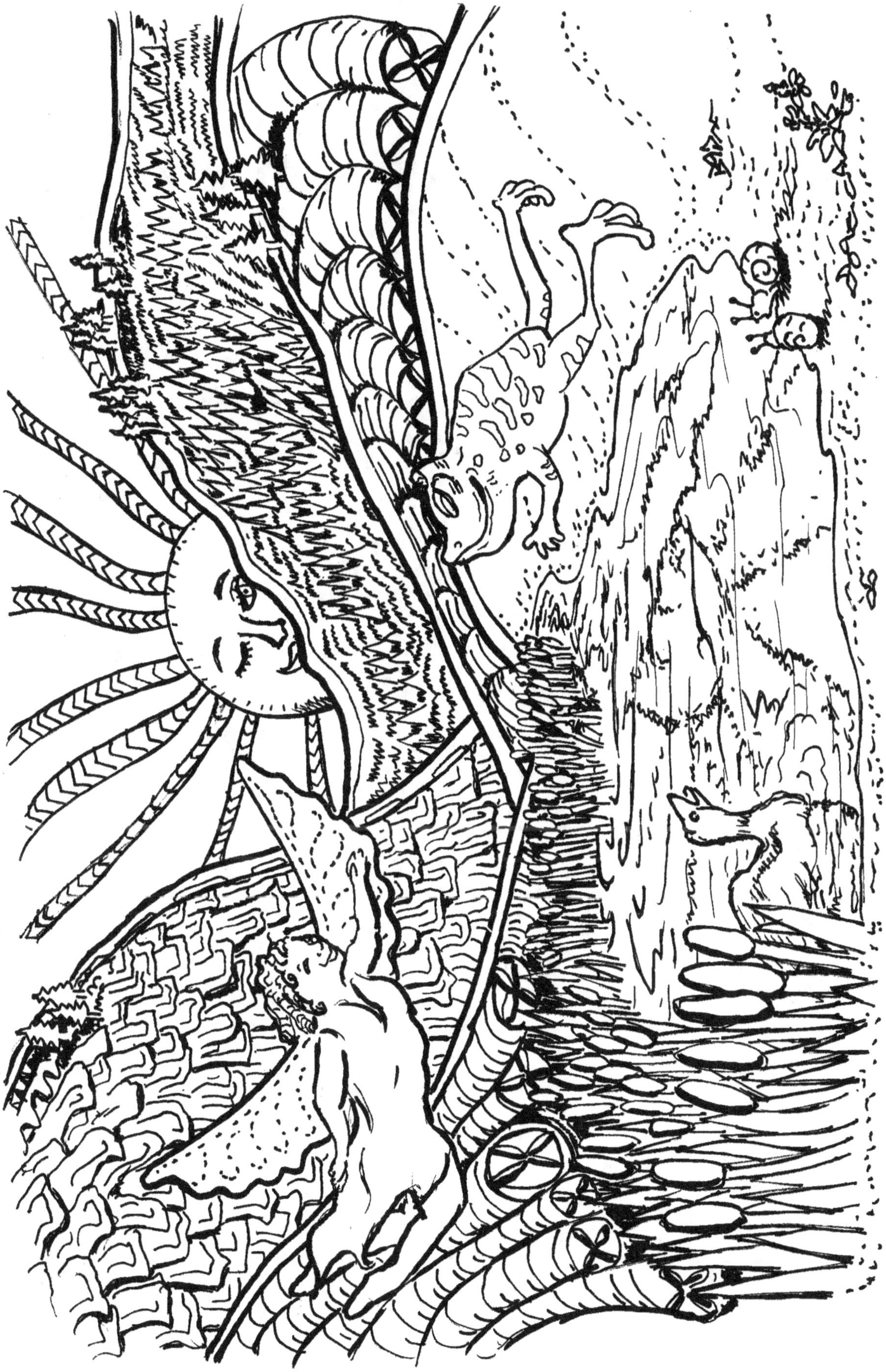

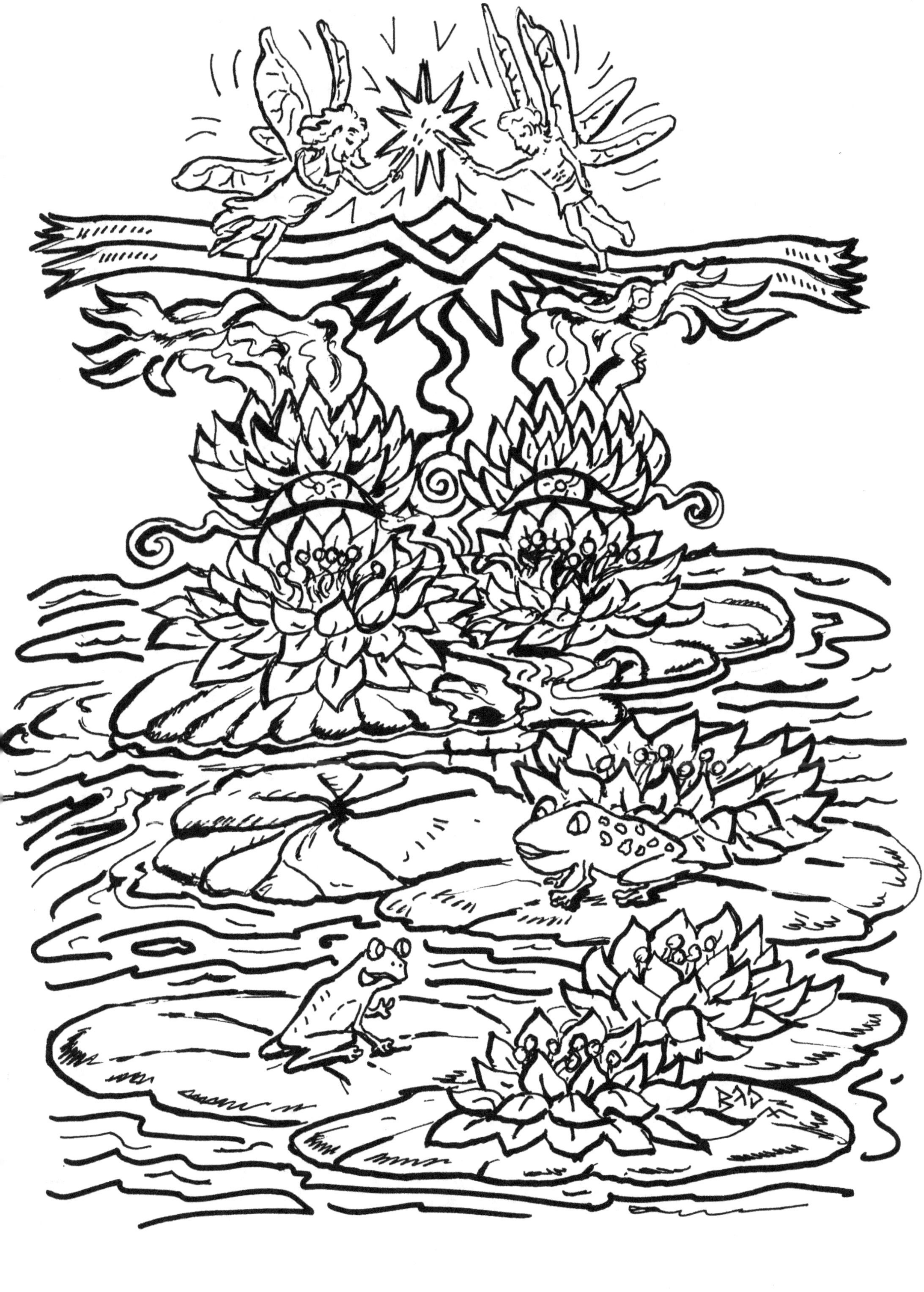

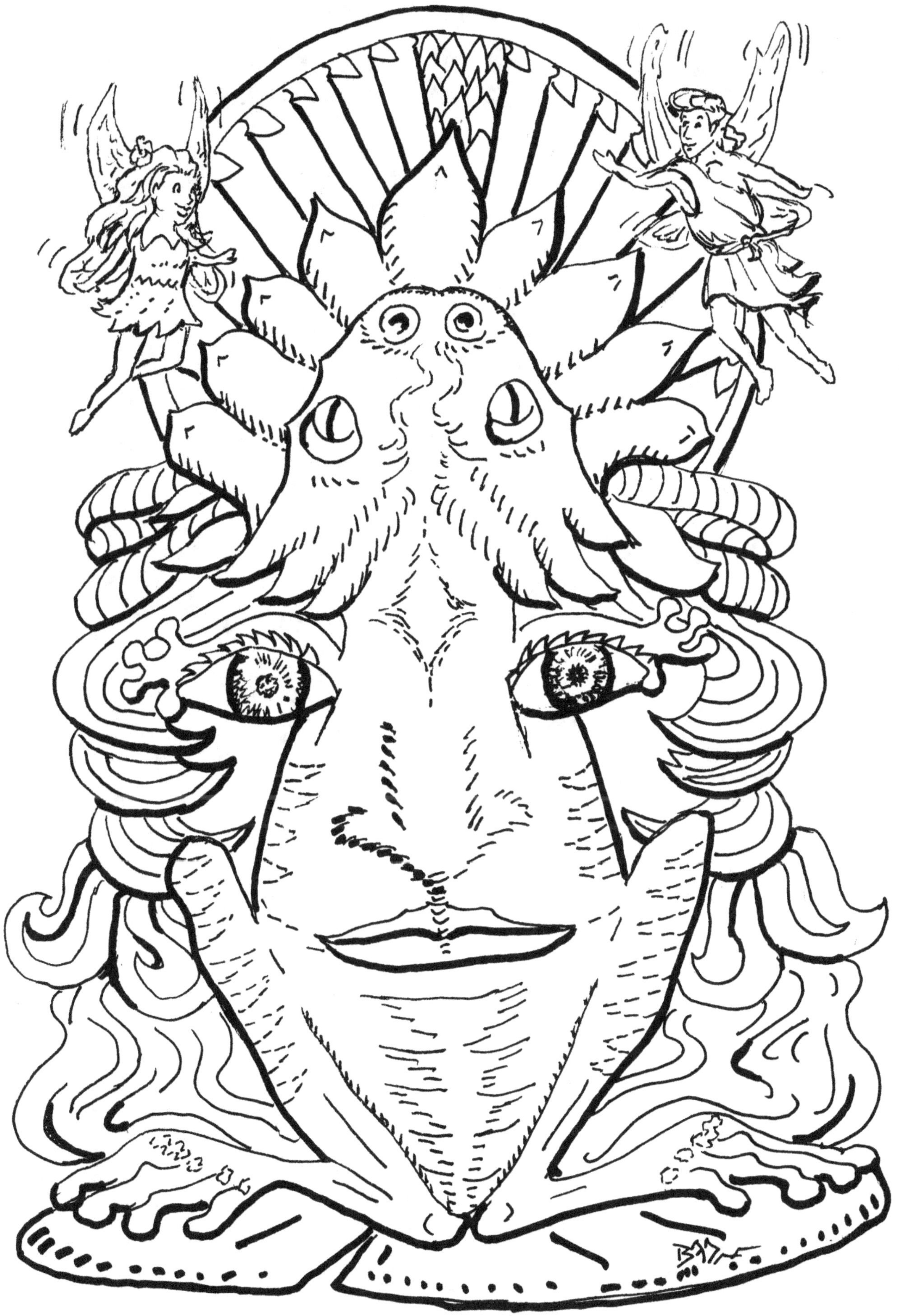

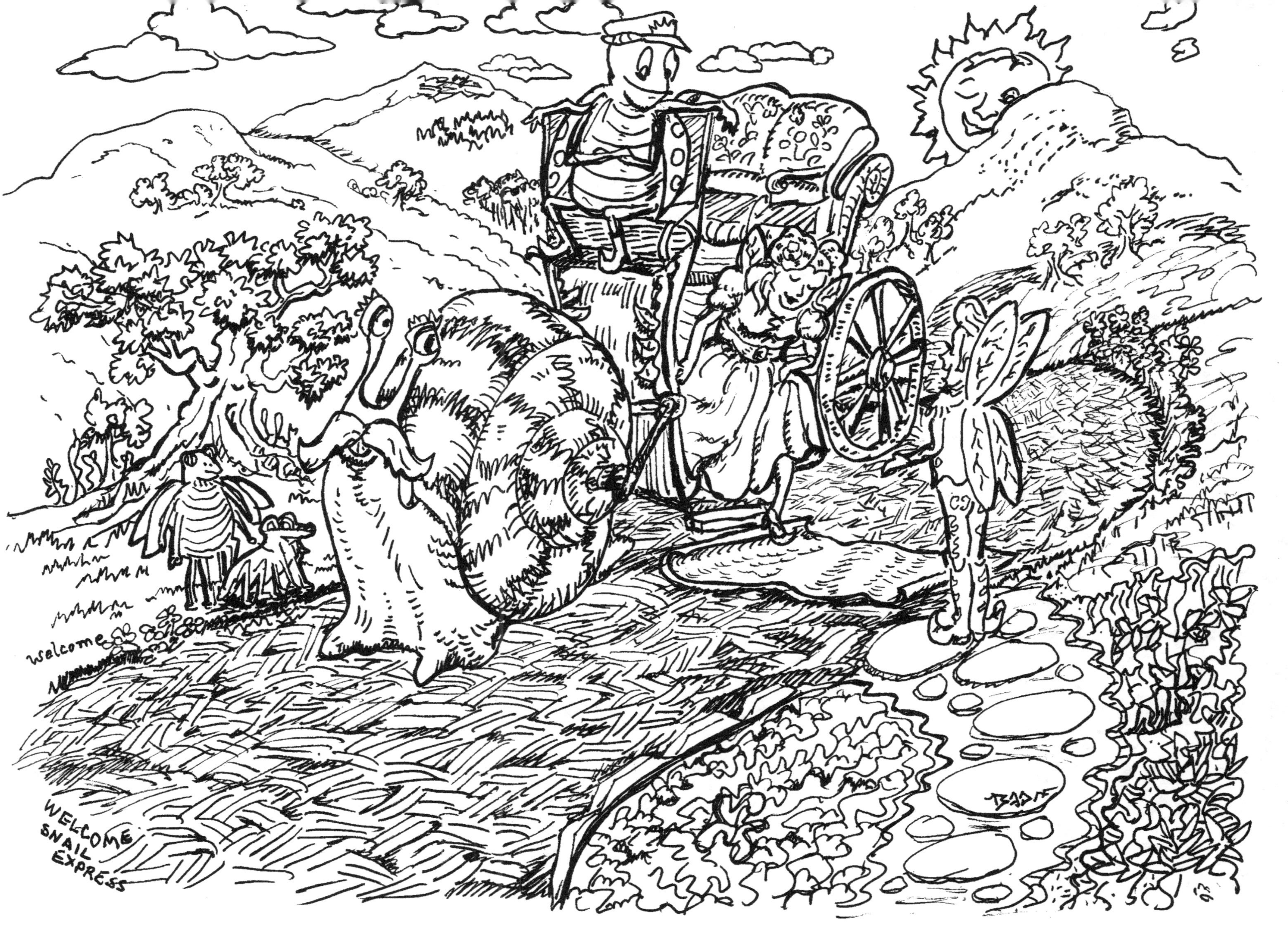
welcome
WELCOME
SNAIL
EXPRESS

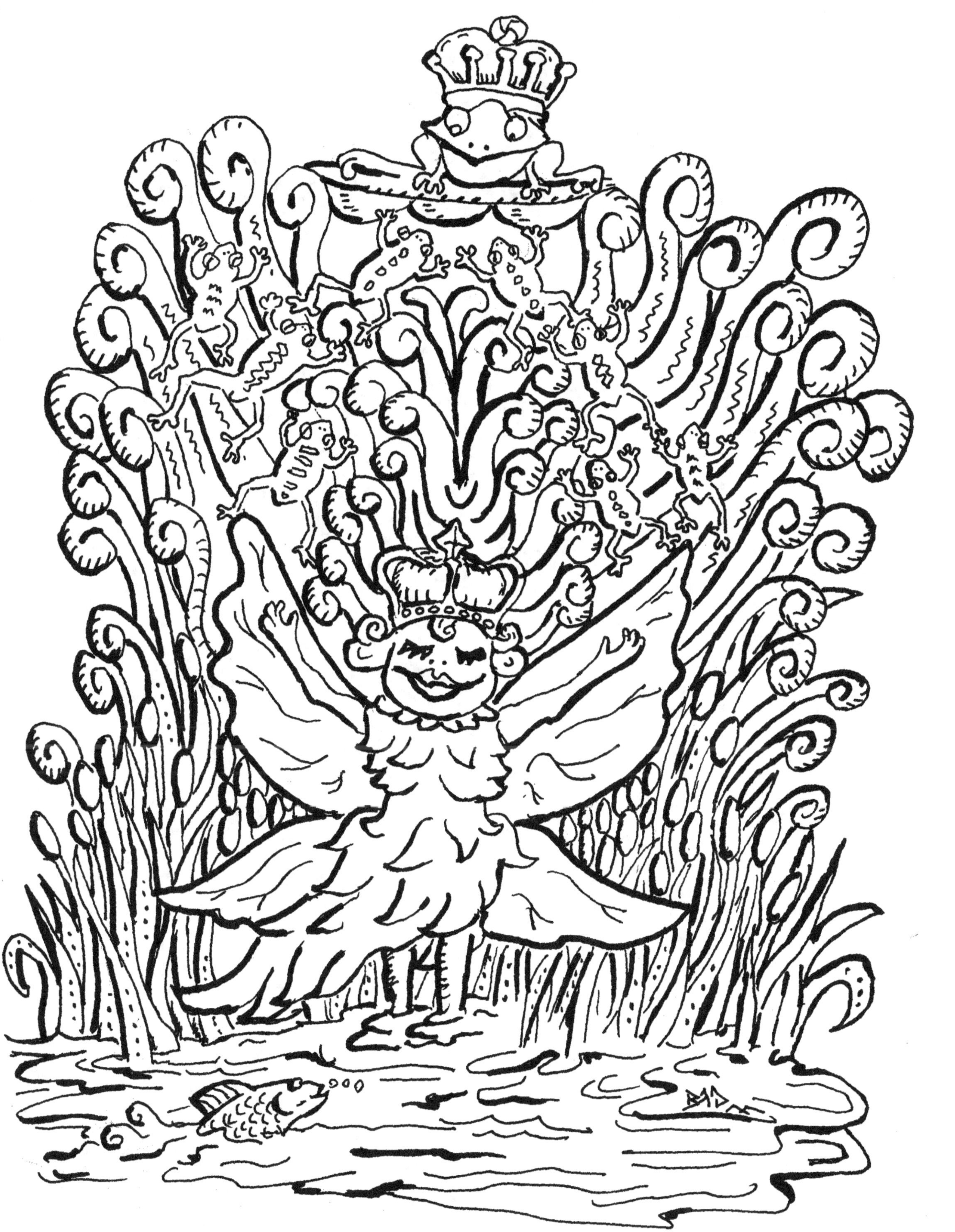

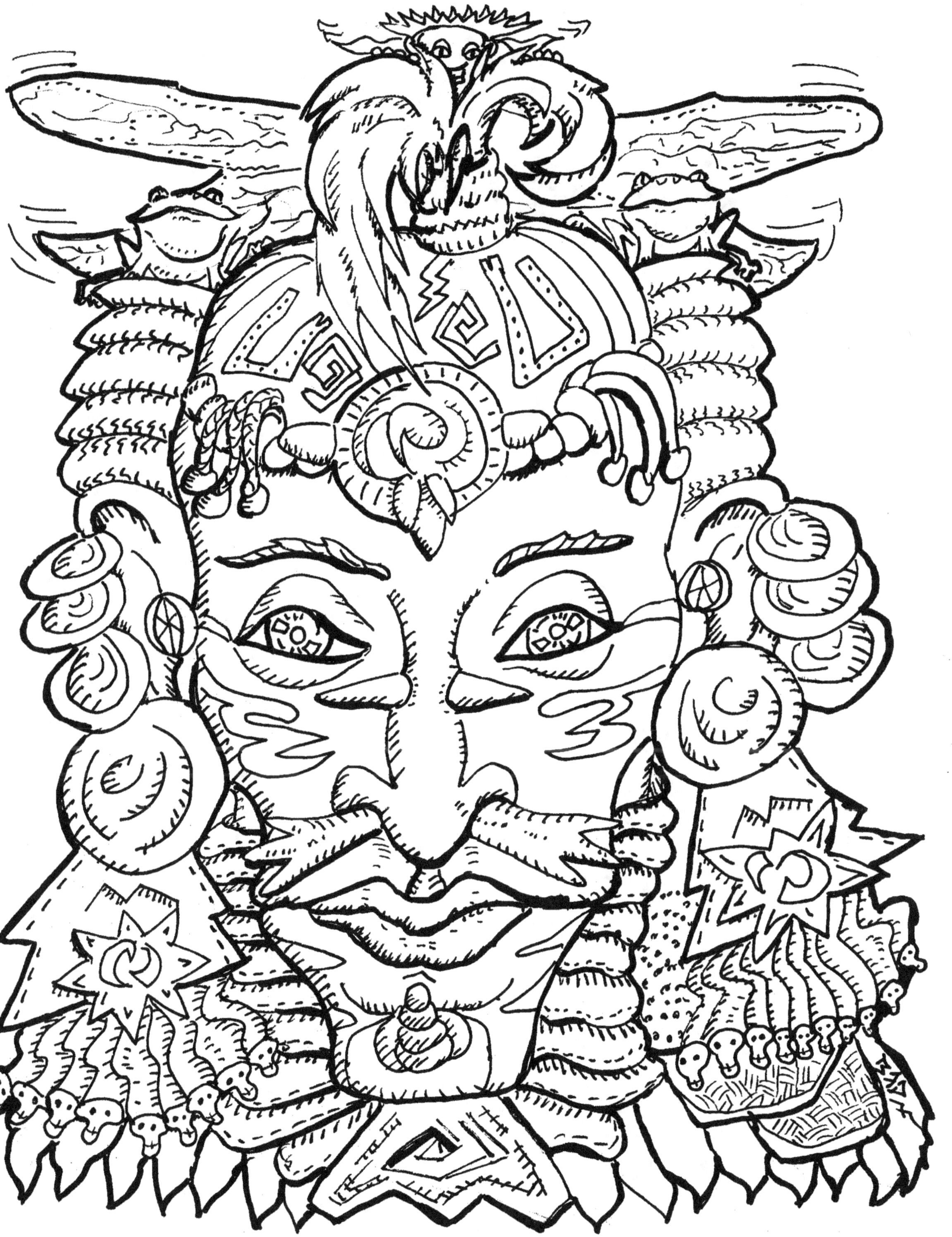

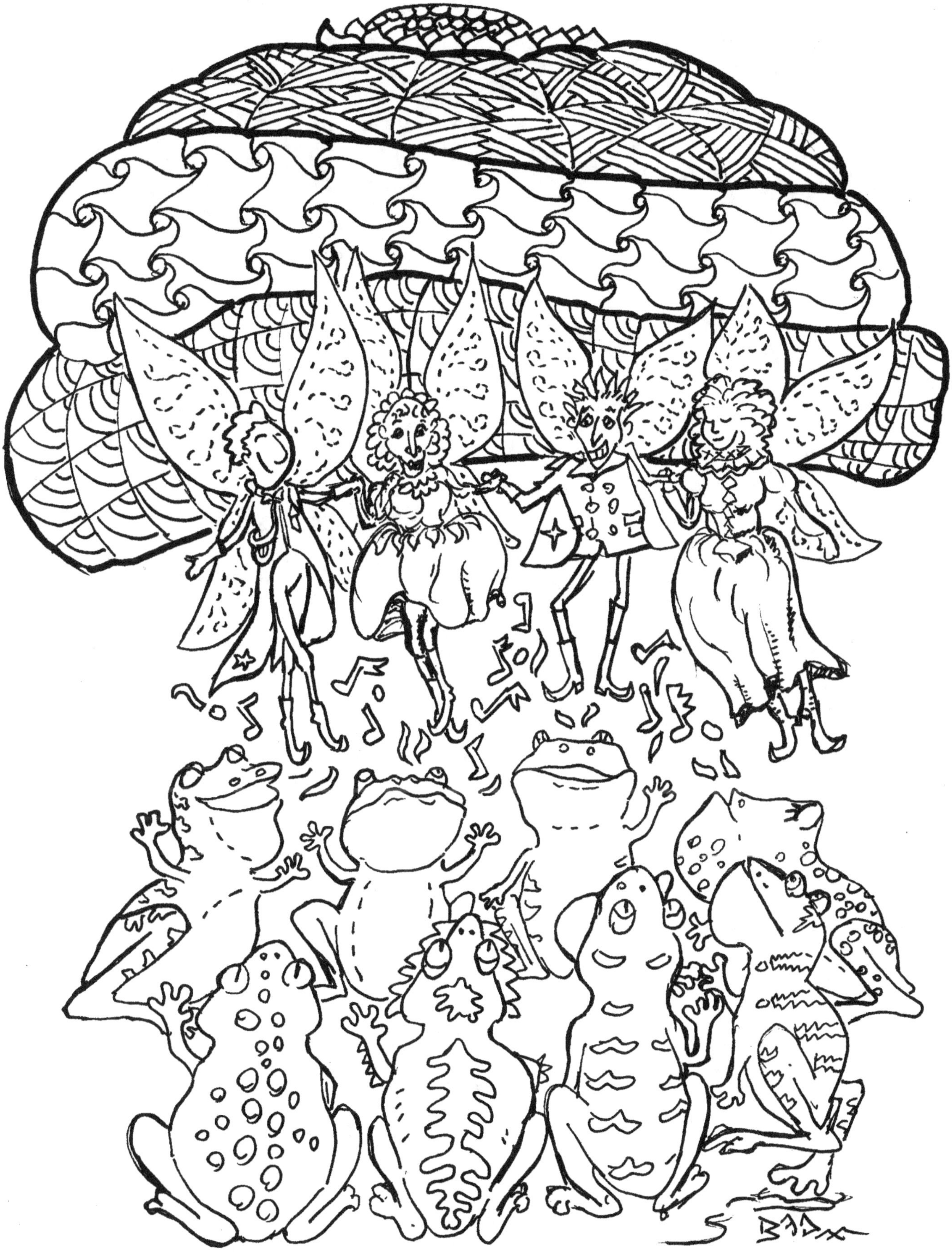

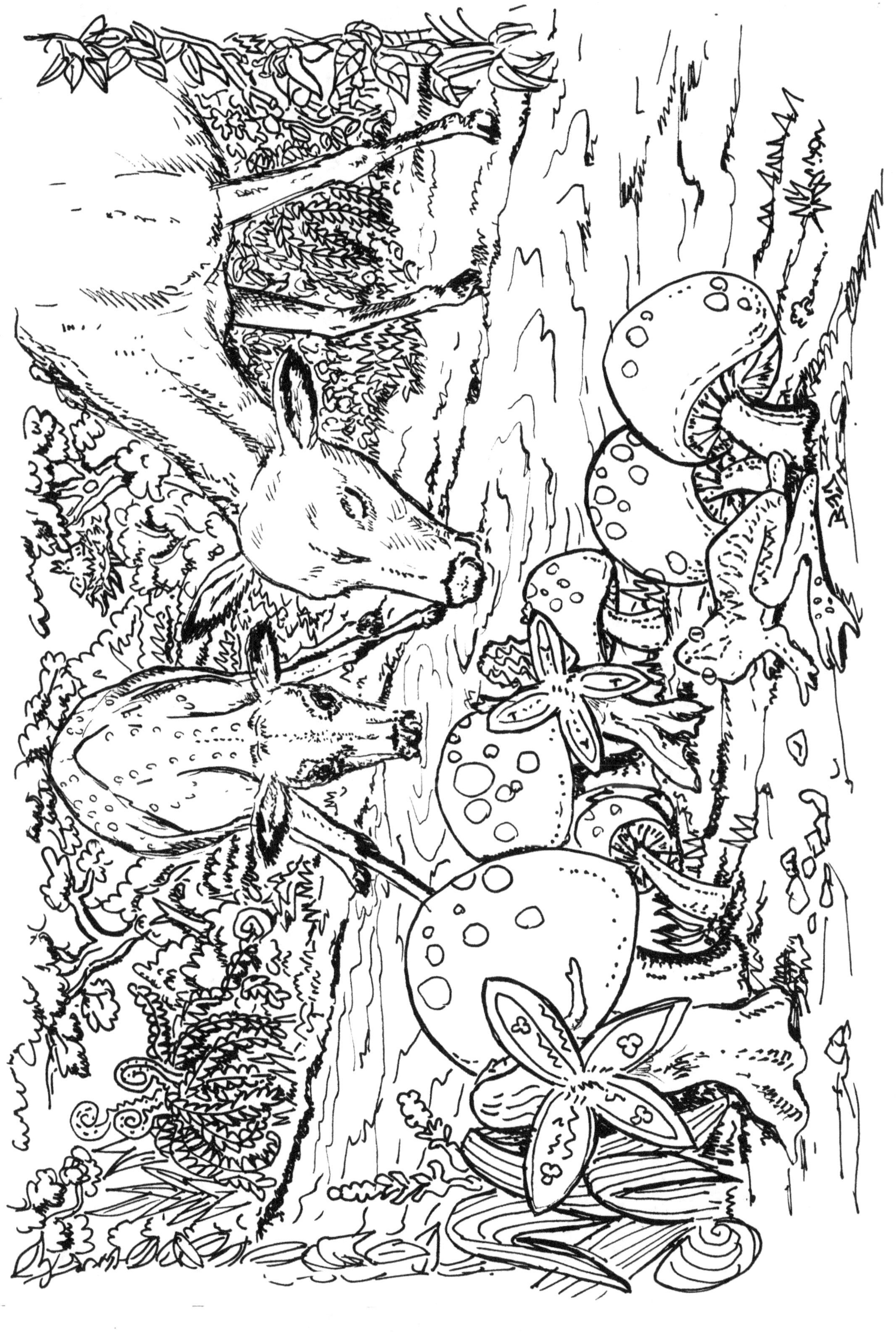

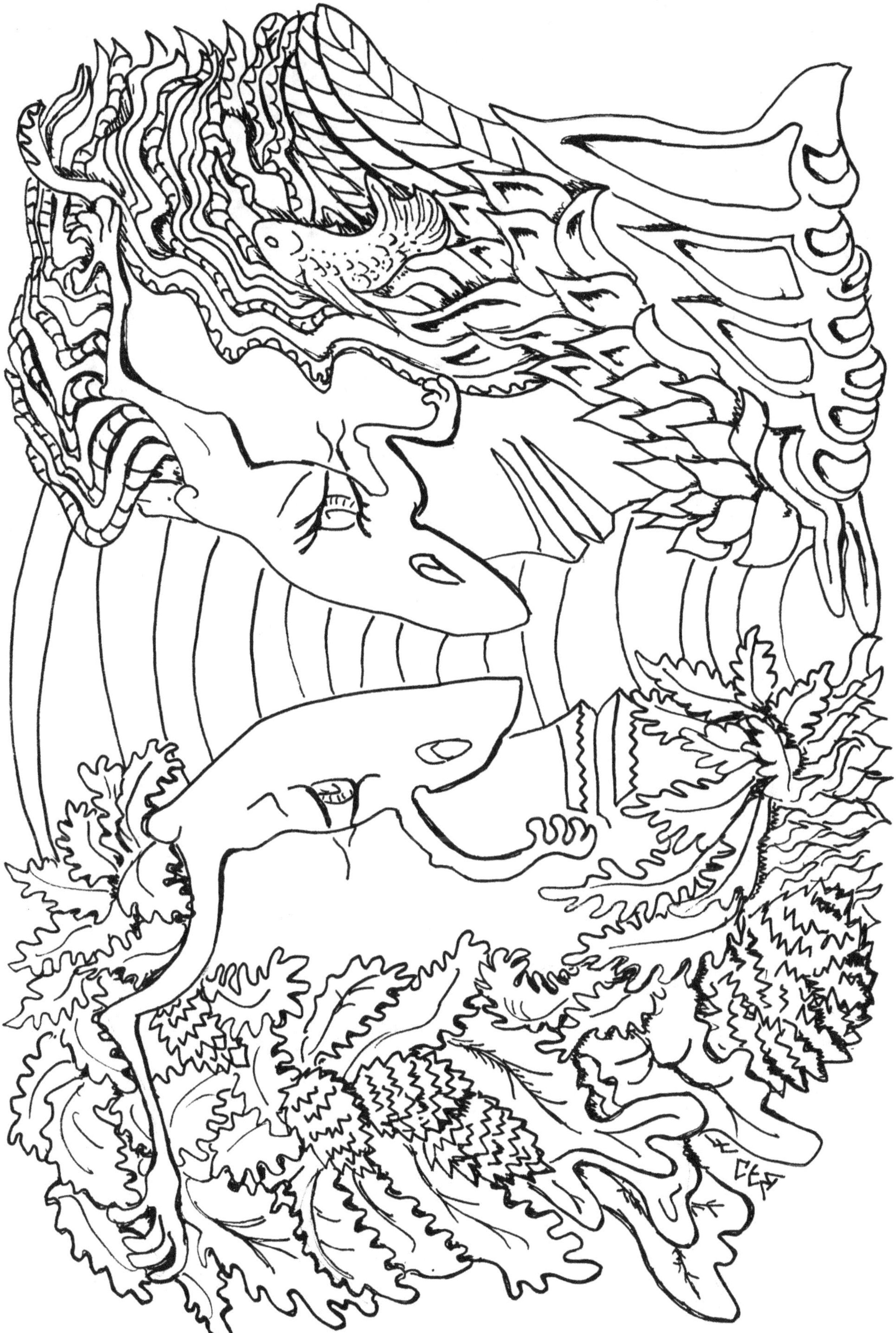

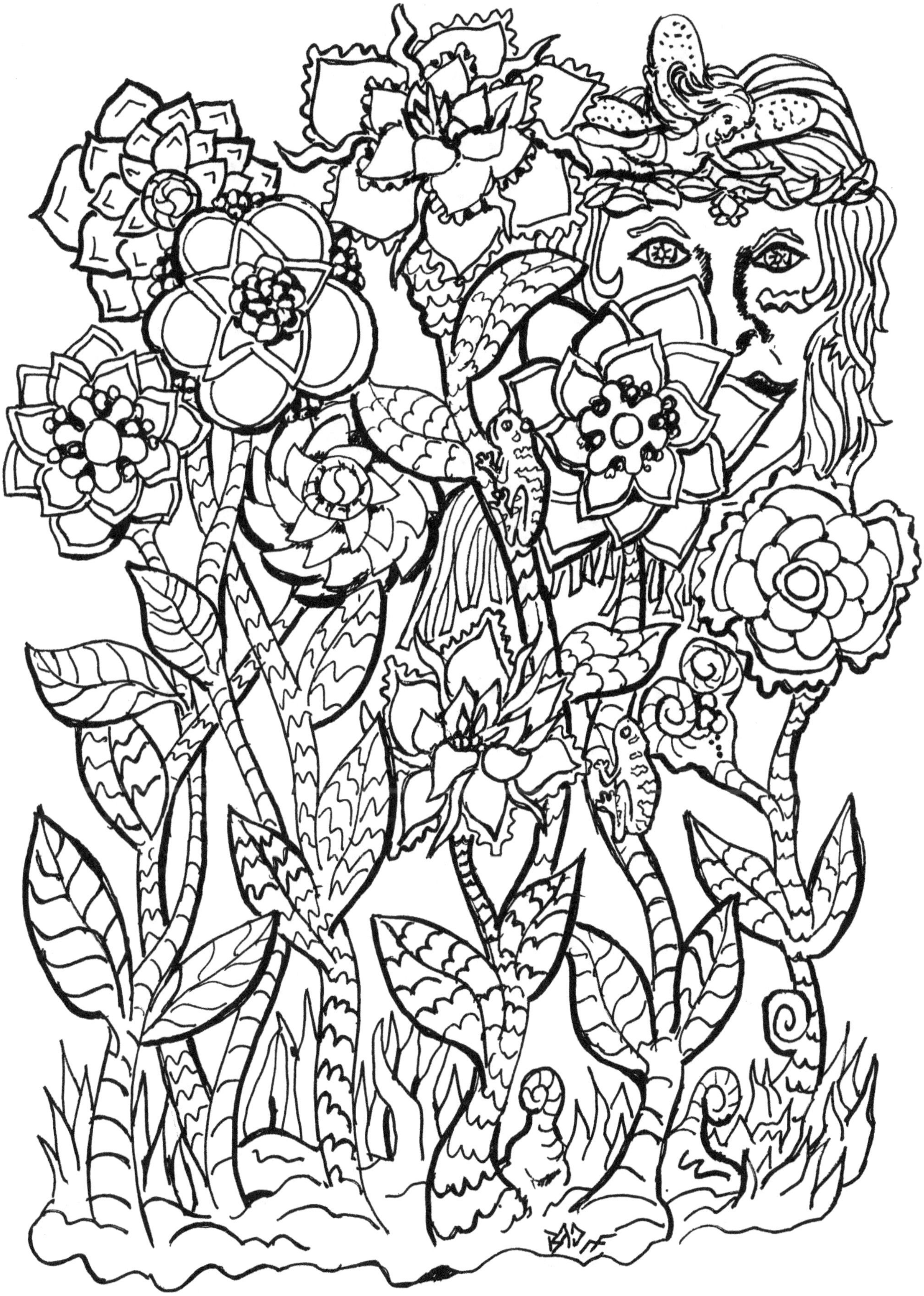

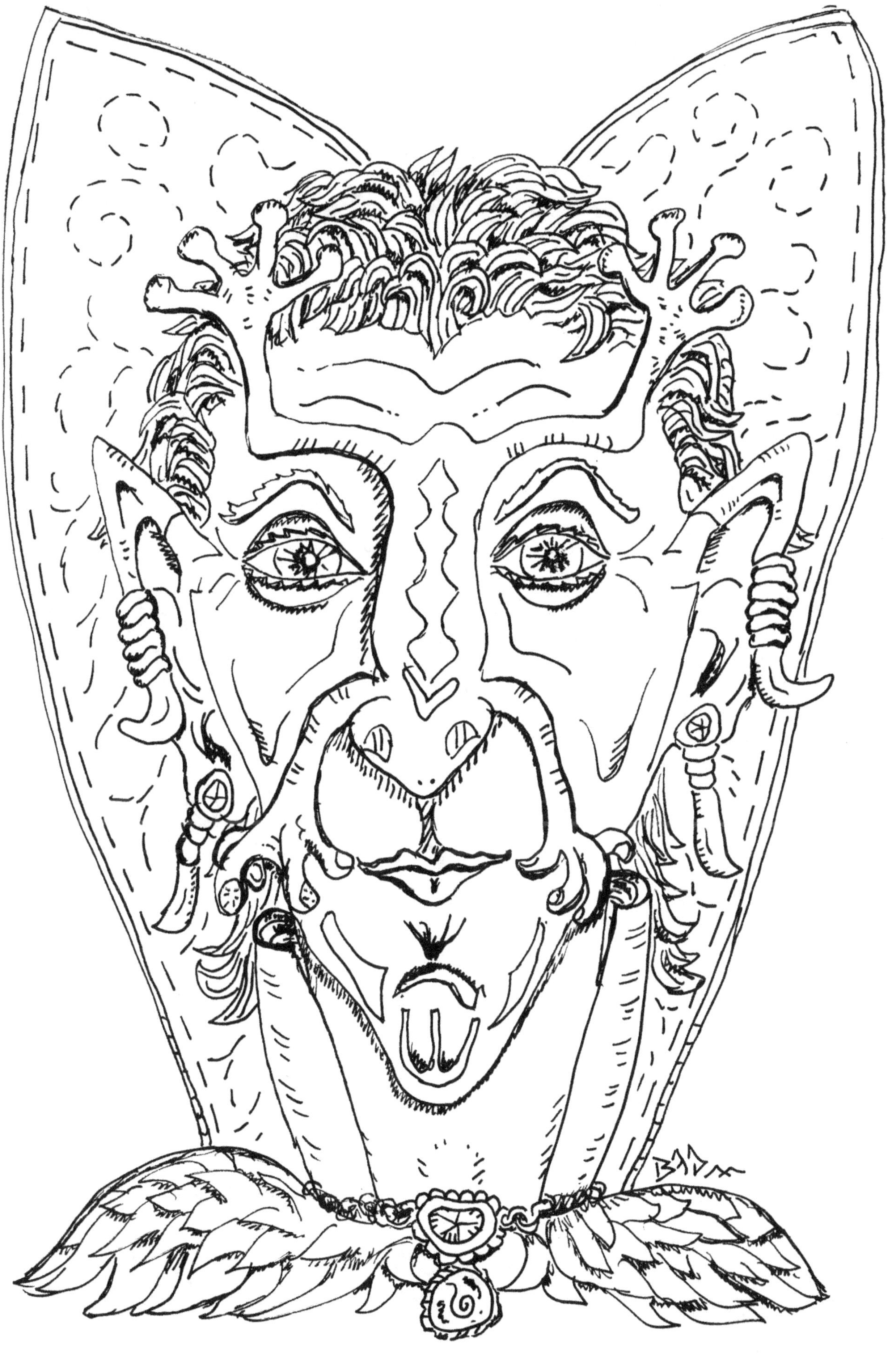

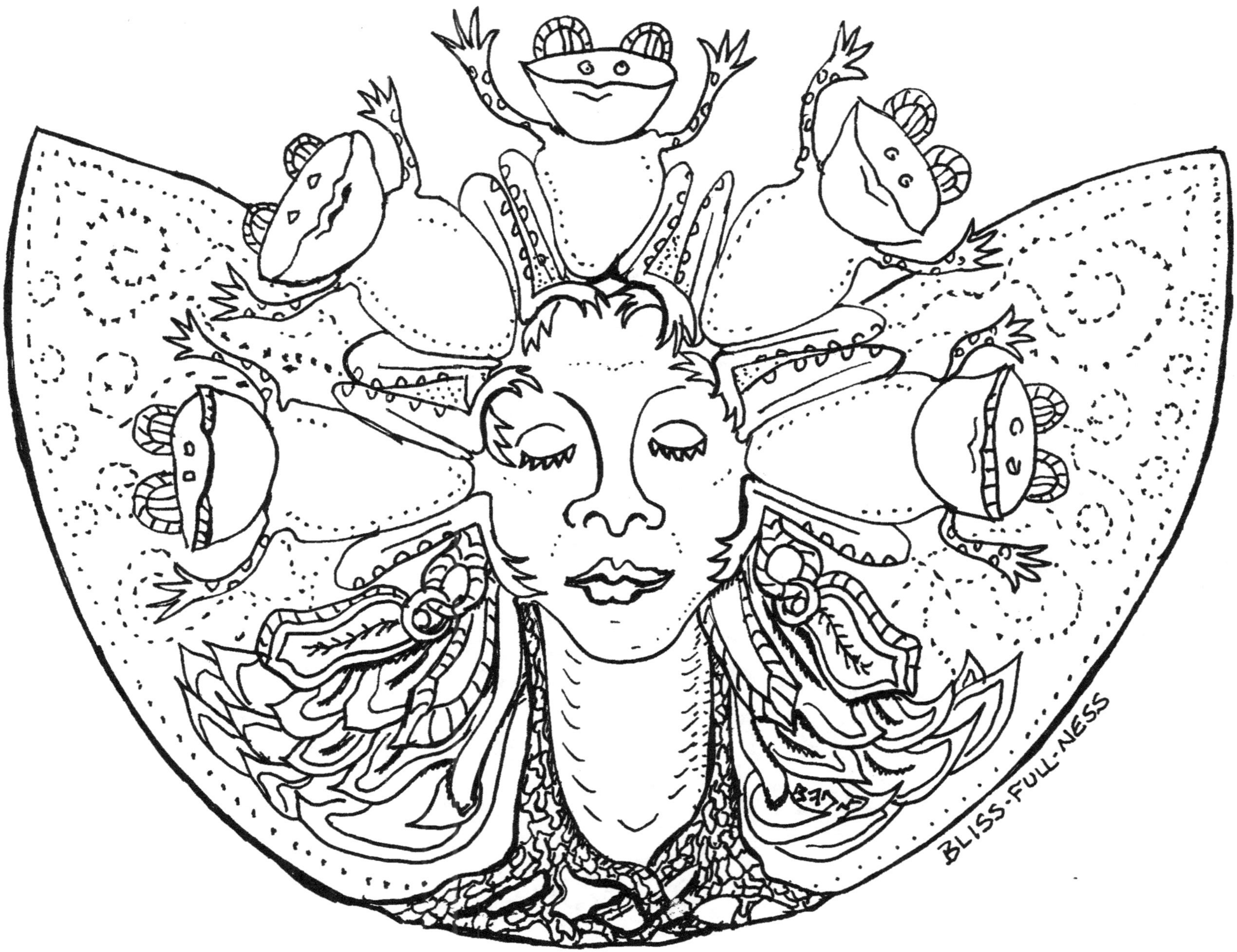
BLISS-FULL-NESS

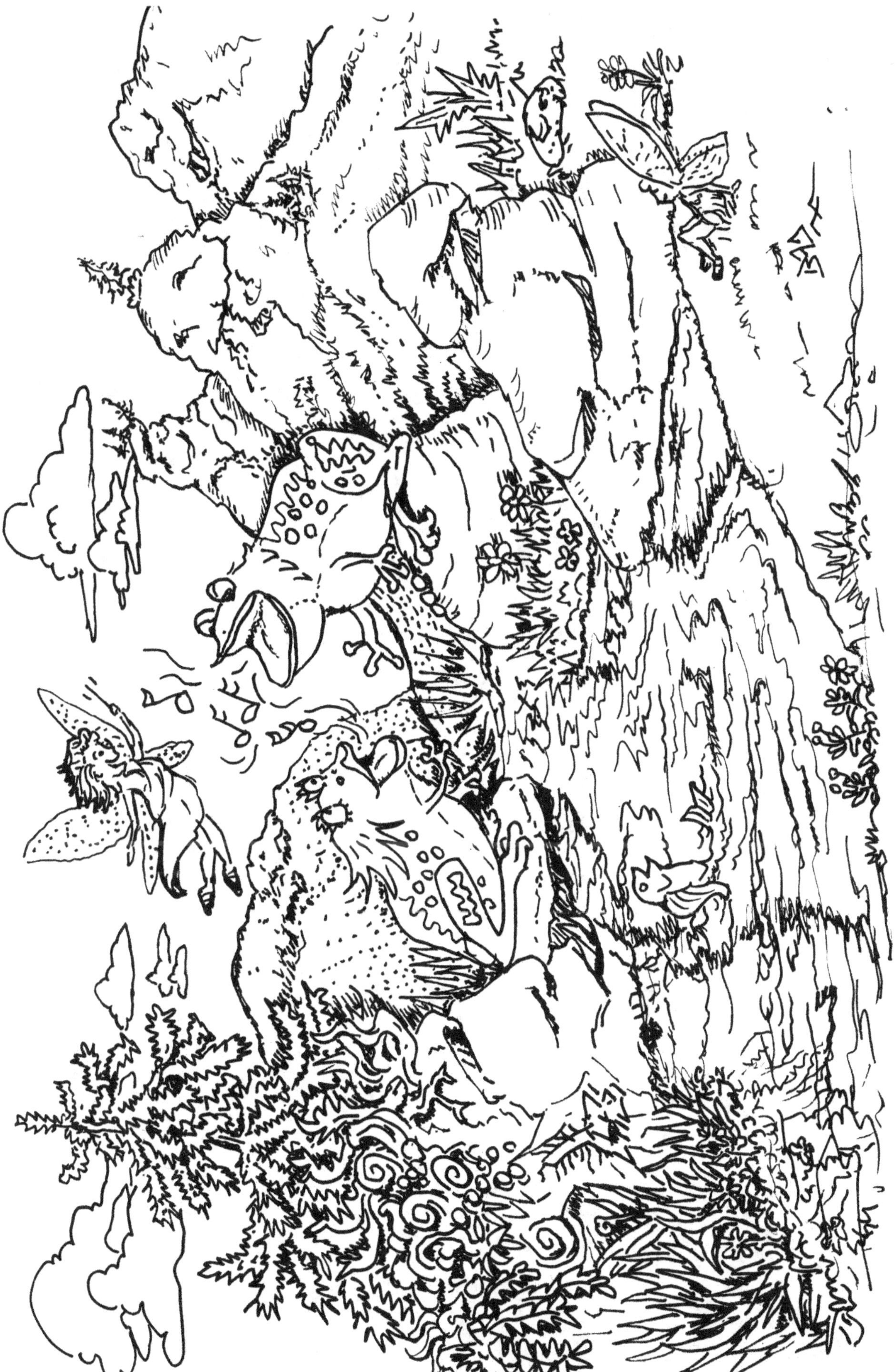

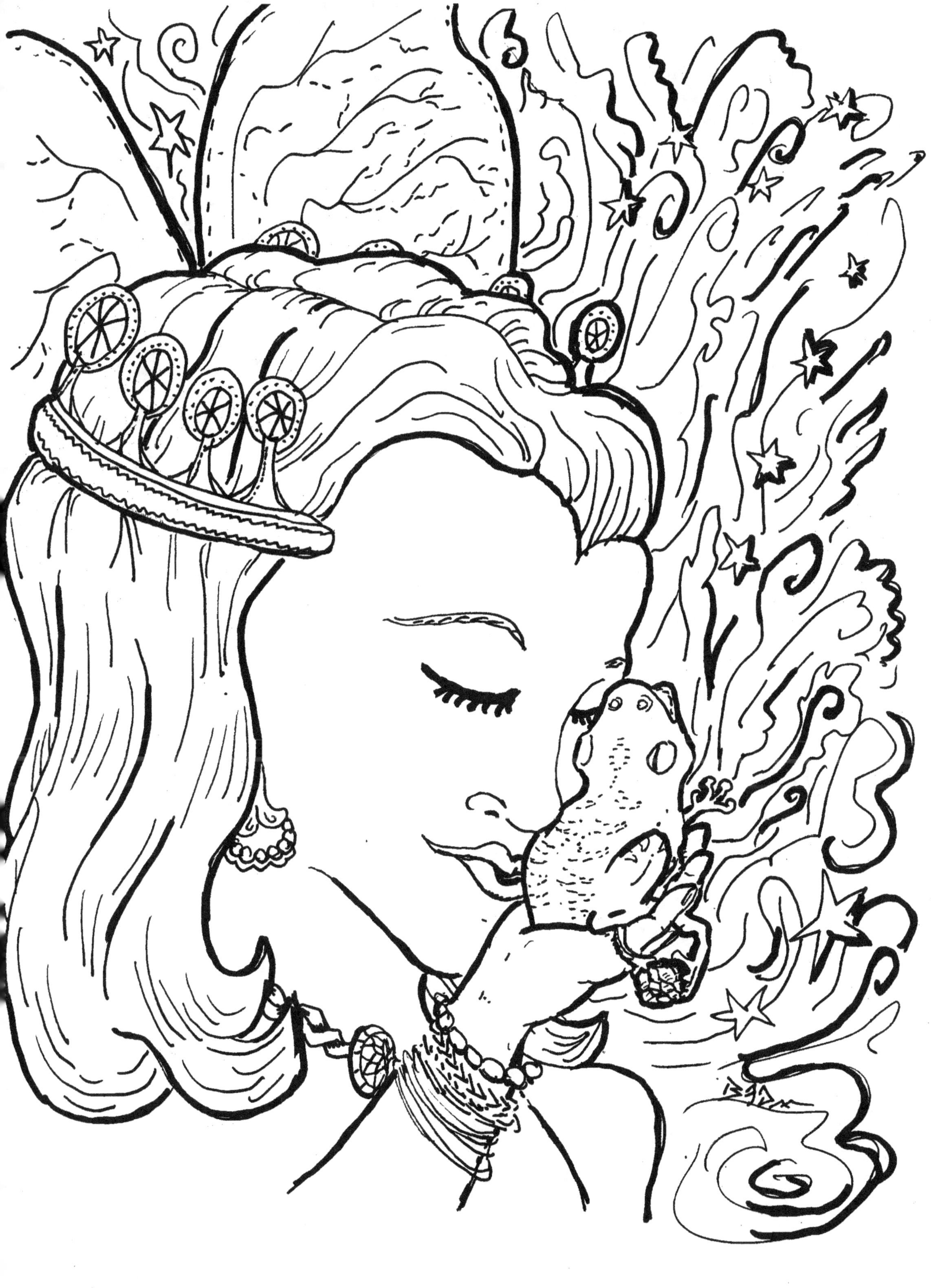

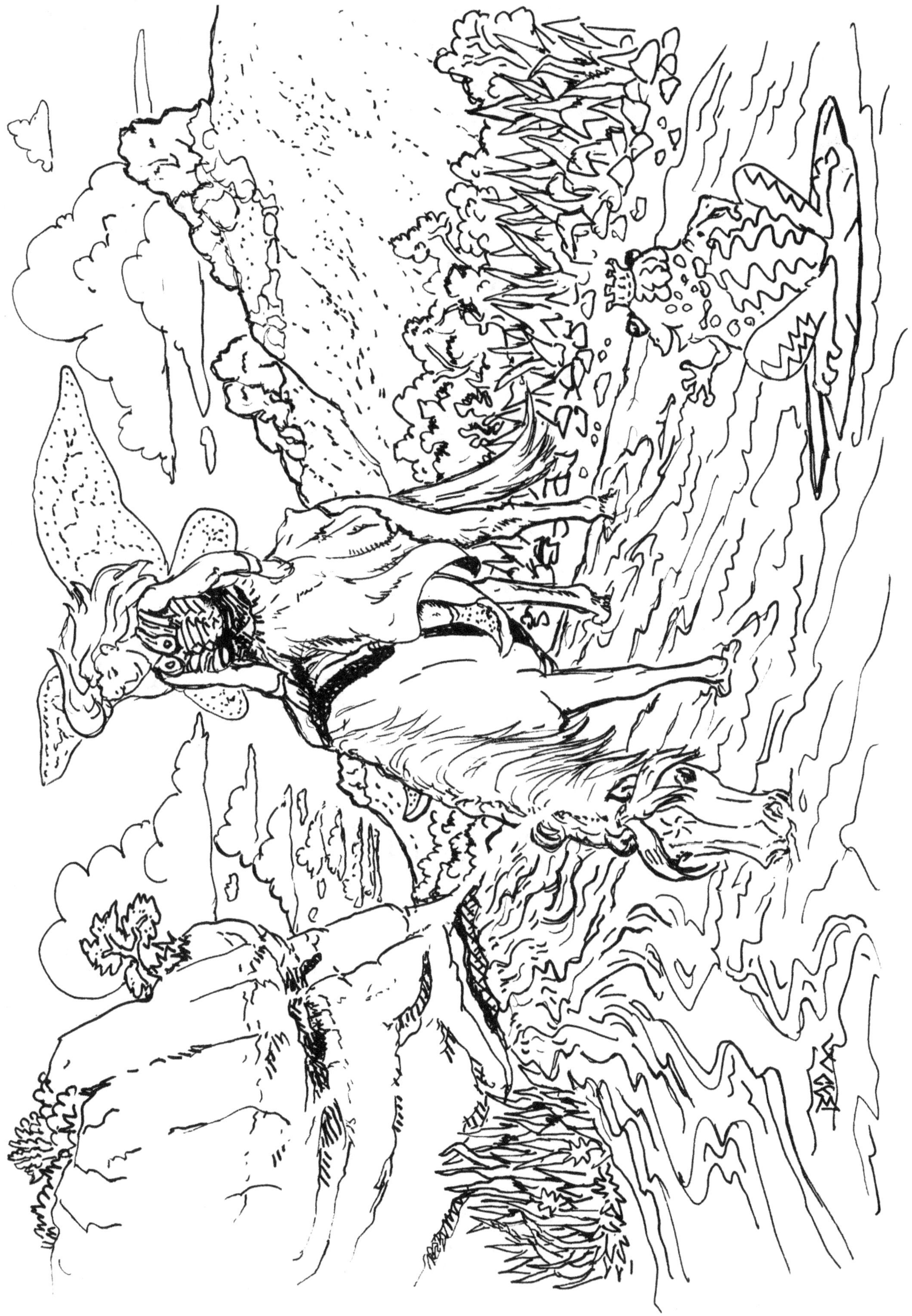

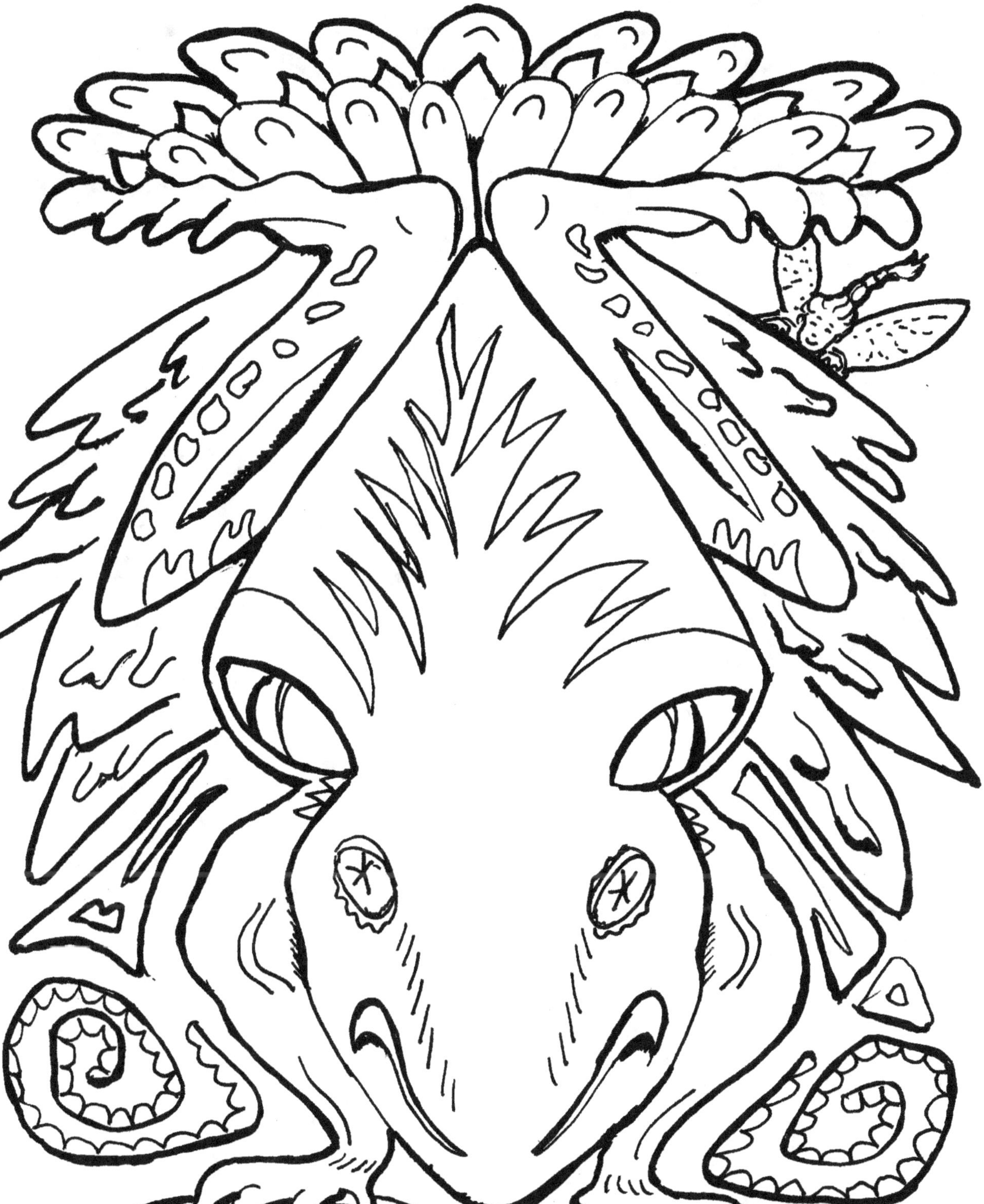

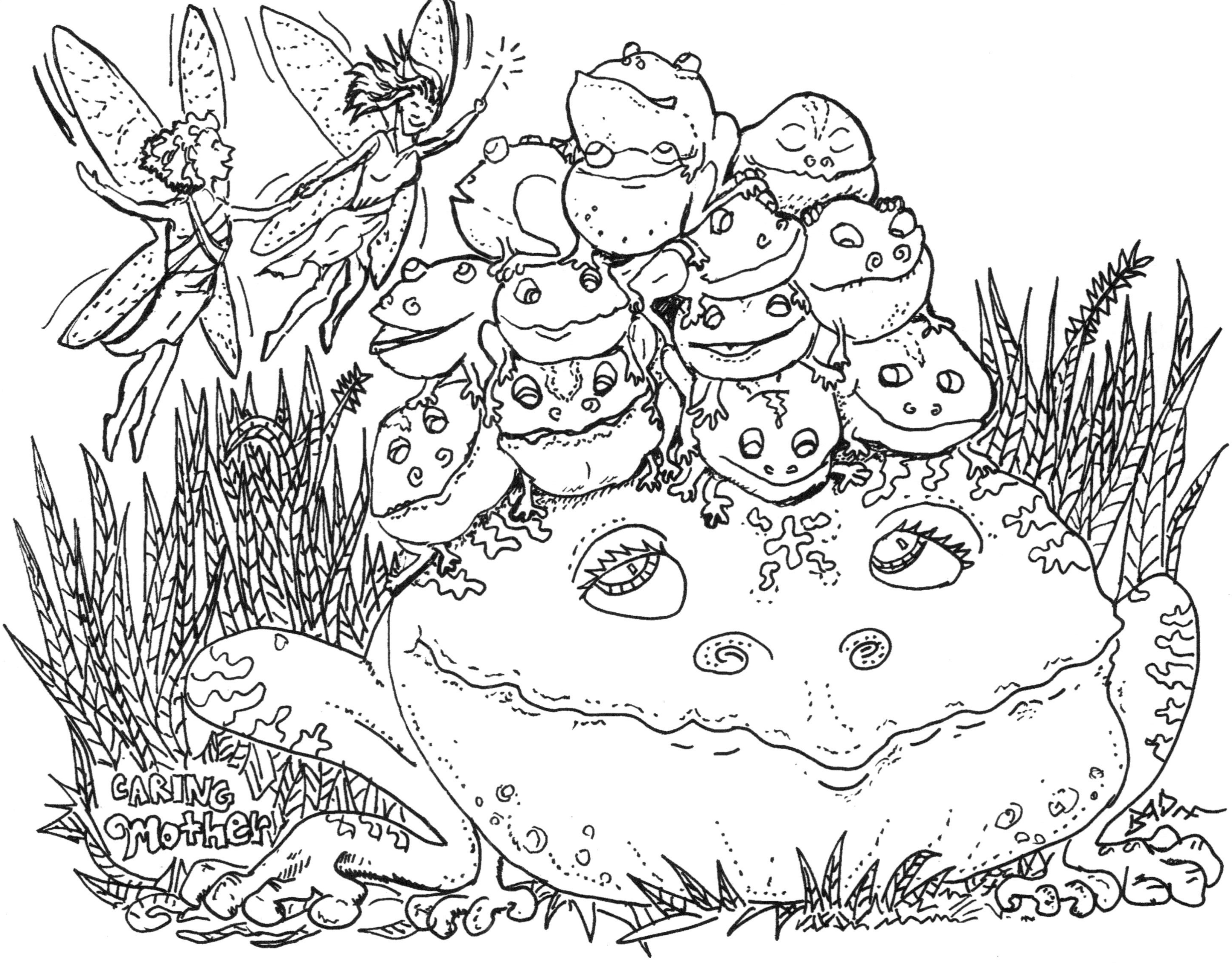
CARING
Mother

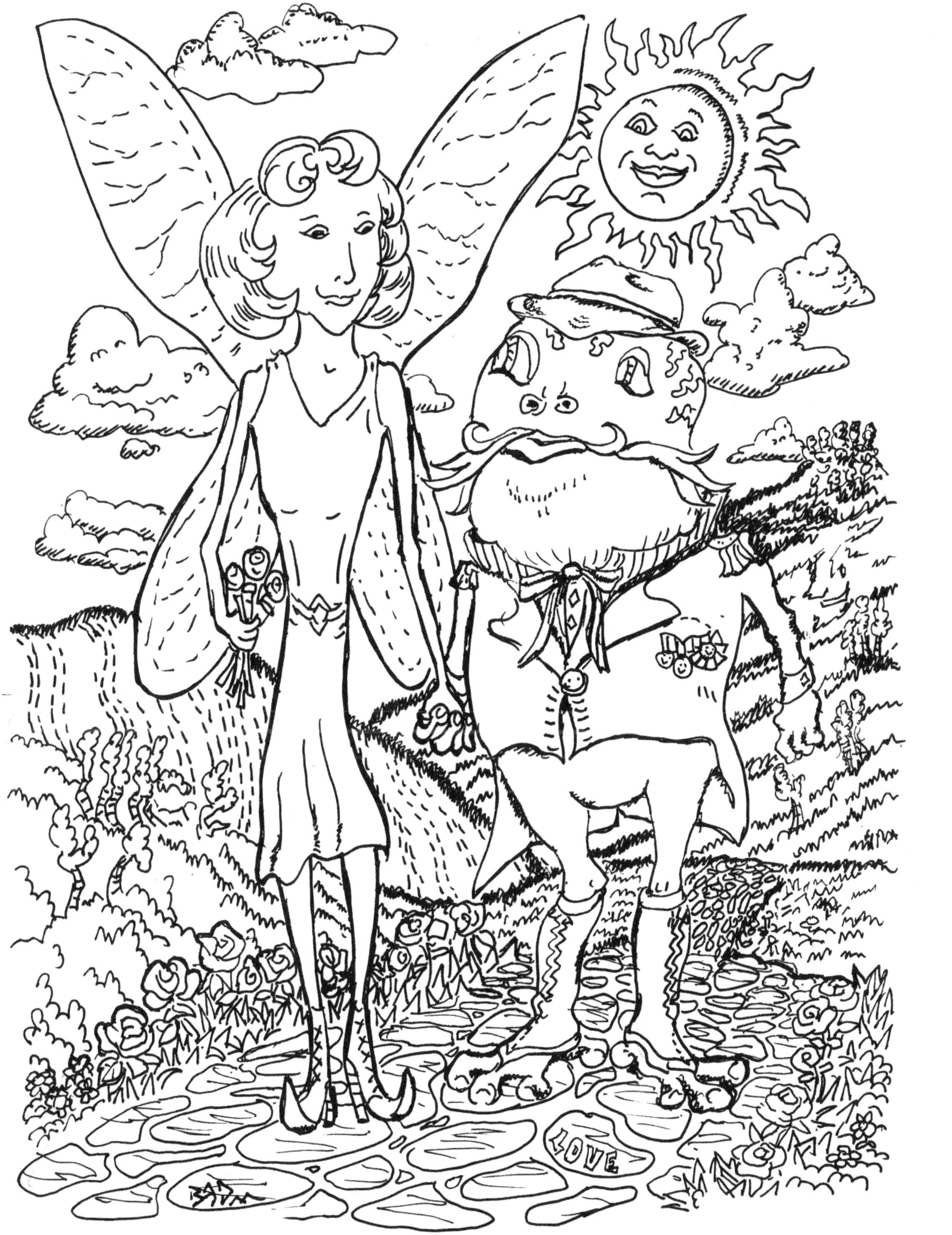
LOVE

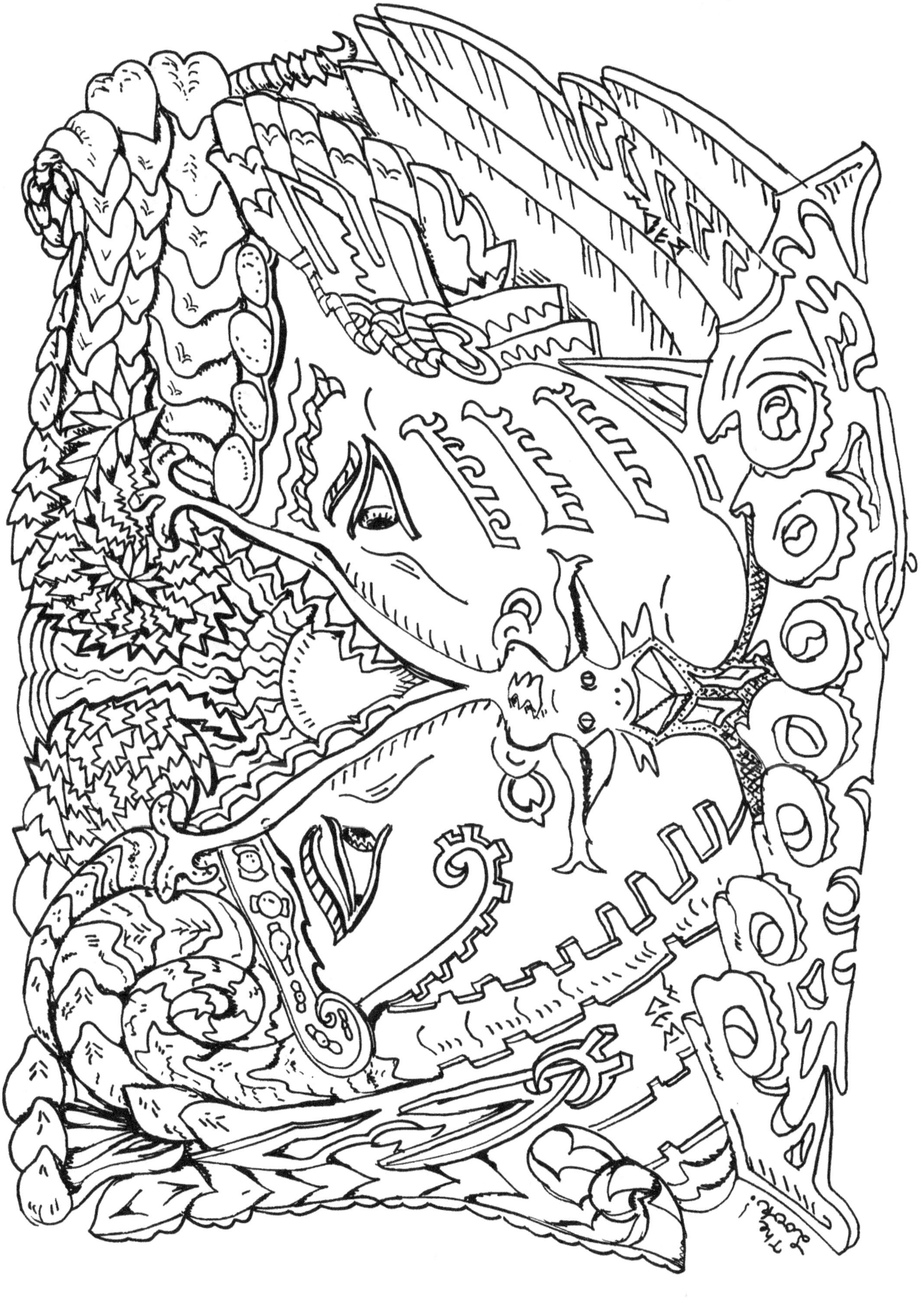

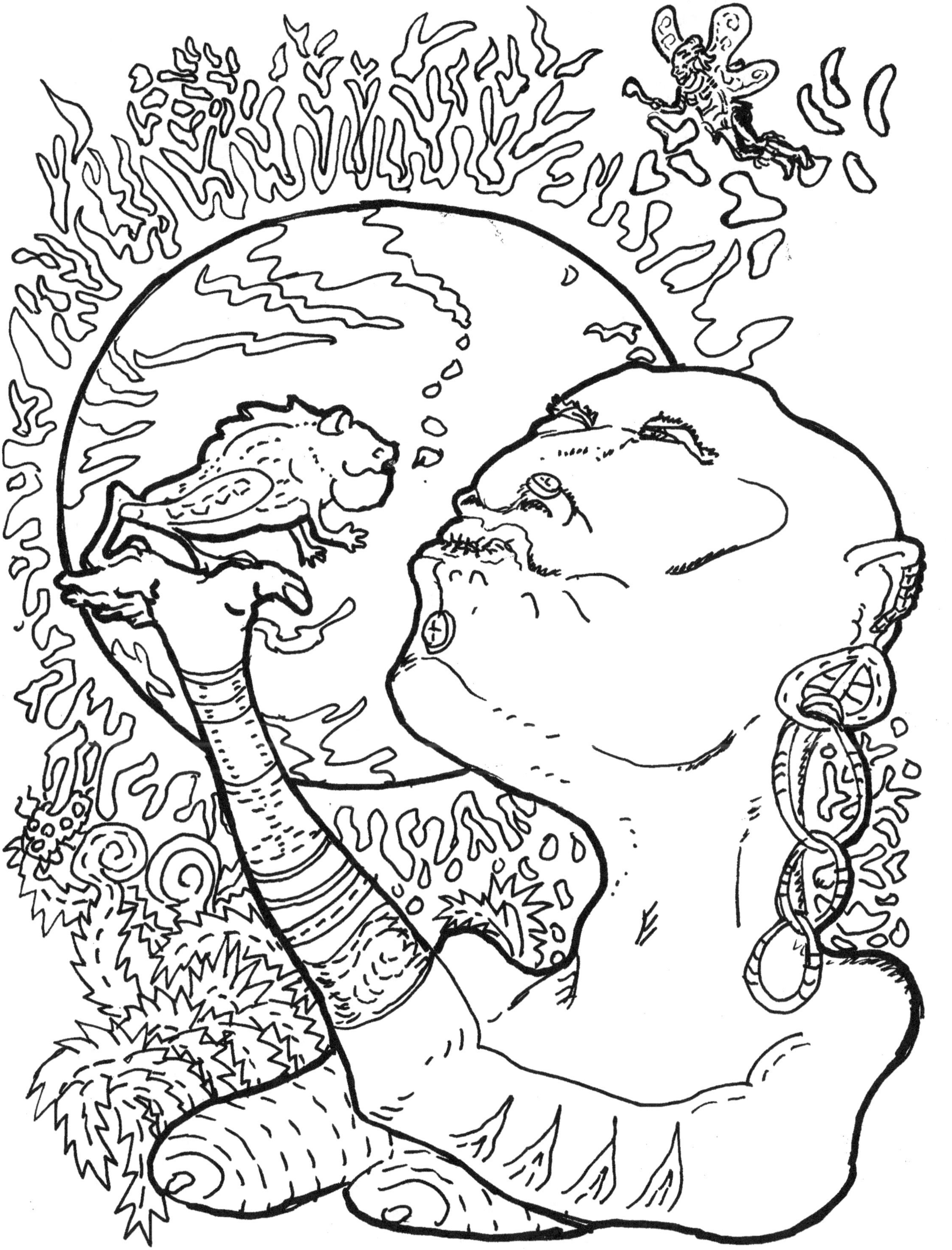

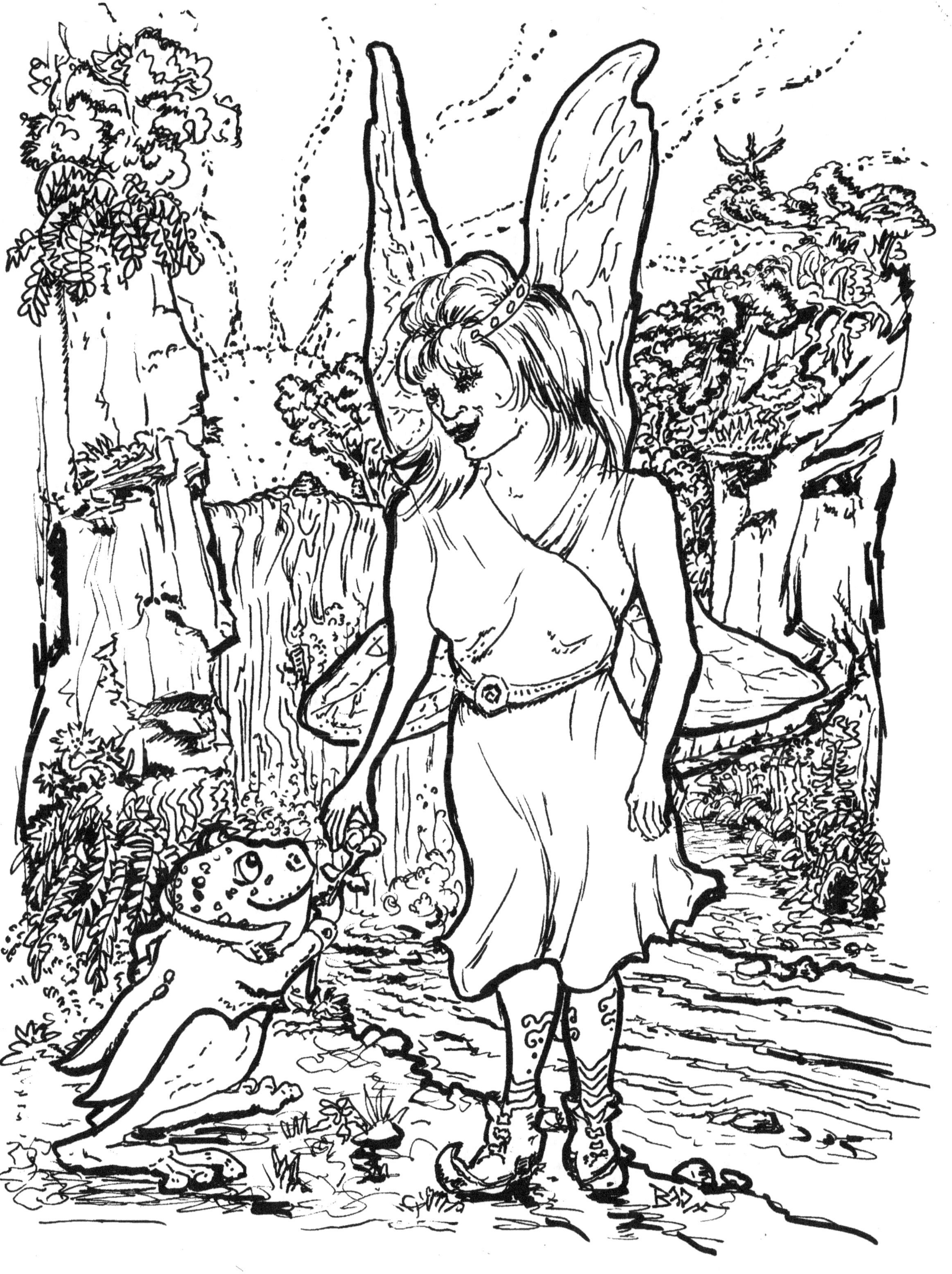

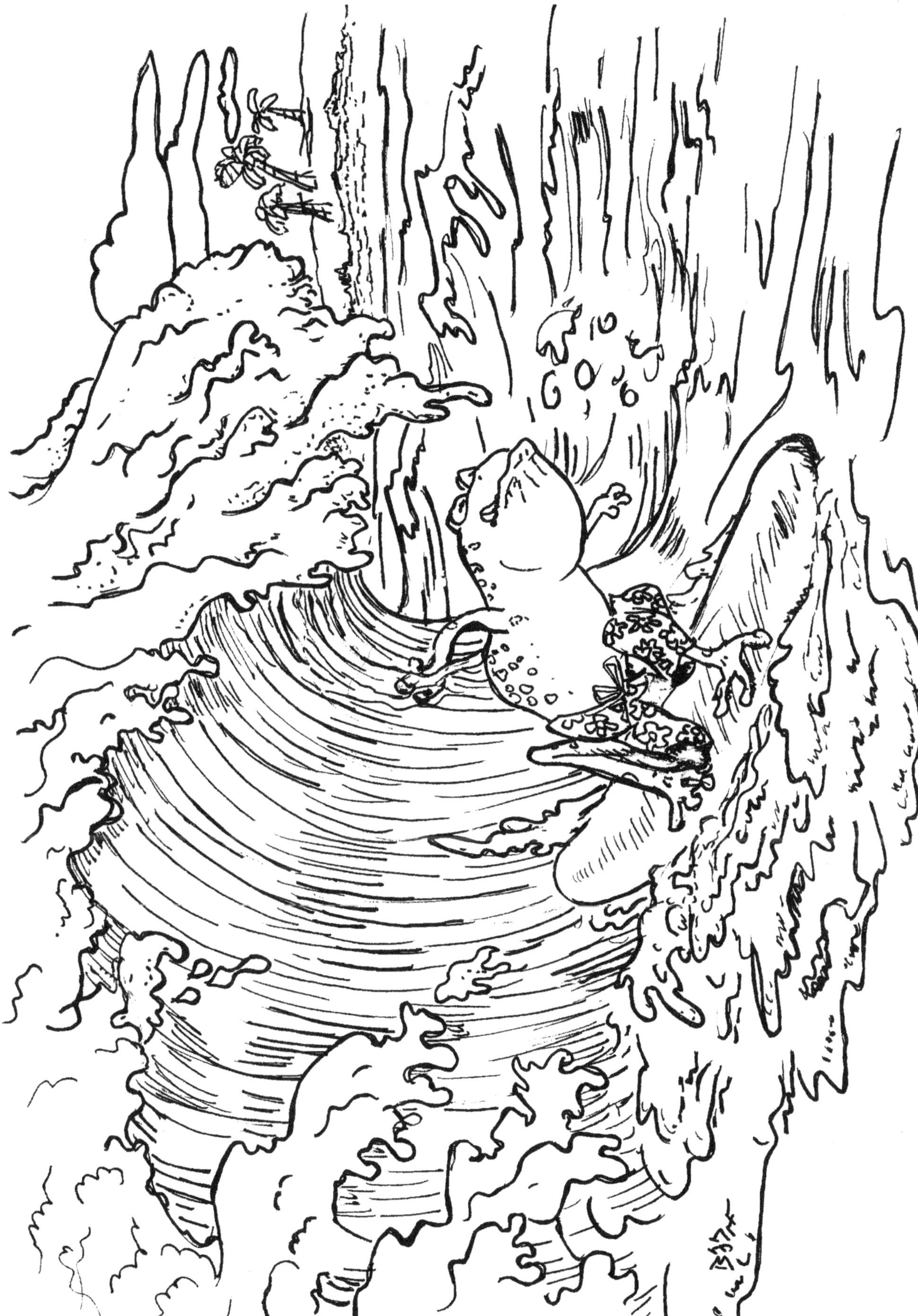

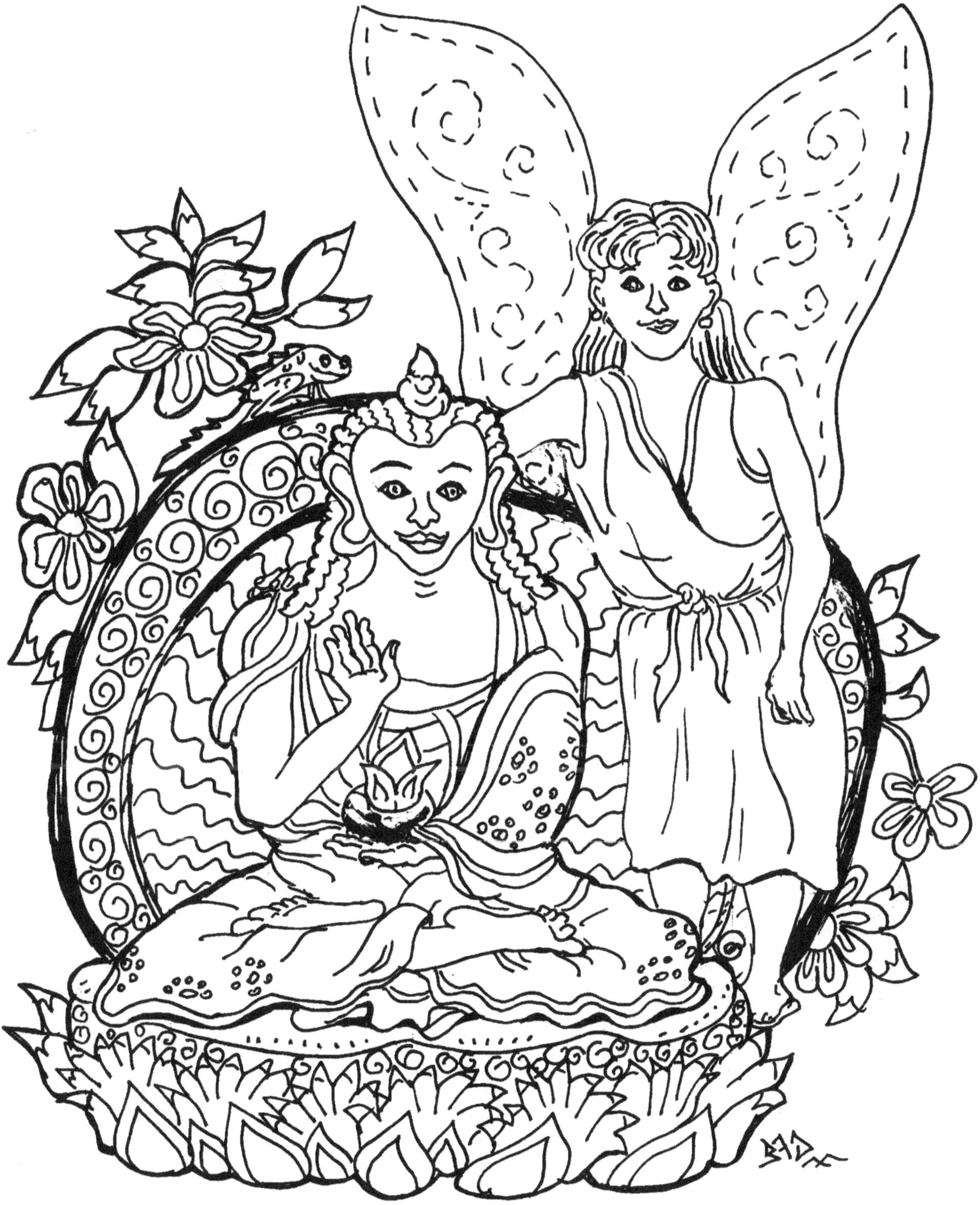

www.ingramcontent.com/pod-product-compliance
Lightning Source LLC
Chambersburg PA
CBHW081305180526
45170CB00007B/2573
* 9 7 8 1 5 4 6 9 4 6 7 9 3 *